Table of Contents

Introduction

A gradual loss of weight in a dog is okay and even beneficial if it is expected or there is an obvious reason for it (such as an increase in exercise or a deliberate change of diet). Unexplained rapid weight loss, however, is a concern and should be checked by your veterinarian as soon as you become aware of it.For example a loss of 2 kg on an average person over a few weeks is generally insignificant.The same amount of weight on a 20 kg dog equates to 10% of their body weight and may indicate an underlying disease process.

What Is A Healthy Weight Range For Your Dog?

There are some useful charts available that are a helpful guide to know the ideal weight for your pet.

Please note: there can be significant variation between genetic lines within each breed and it can be difficult to predict the ideal weight of a cross-bred dog due to the presence of 2 or more breeds in its lineage.

The easiest way to assess your dog's ideal weight is to follow a few simple steps:

- Regularly run your hands over your dog's ribs. Can you feel their ribs easily or is there a significant layer of fat over the ribs?

- Observe your dog from above. Can you see a definite waist line or does it blend in to the hips?

- Observe your dog from the side. Can you see a waist line or is there a straight line from the chest to the back legs?

- Weigh your dog at least twice a year (your veterinary clinic will be more than happy for you to use their scales, and we can then record your dog's weight at the same time)

All of the above aspects are jointly used to determine a 'body condition score'. Your veterinary team will be able to advise you on the ideal weight for your dog once the condition score is assessed. As indicated below, the ideal condition score is a 3.

What Should You Do If You Notice Your Pet Has Suddenly Lost Weight?

As soon as you notice a loss in weight, especially over a short period of time it is important to get your dog checked by your veterinarian.

Some things to think about prior to your visit that may assist your veterinarian in determining the cause of the weight loss include the following questions.

Has There Been Any Change In Your Dog's:

- Appetite (increased or decreased)?
- Drinking habits (increased or decreased)?
- Diet (eg changed brand of food, given any food scraps from the table recently, possibility of eating any foreign objects)?
- Faeces (eg any vomiting or diarrhoea)?
- Urination (increased frequency or any difficulty in urinating)?
- Behaviour (eg lethargic, sleepy, restless or hyperactive)?
- Mobility (eg difficulty in walking or getting up after resting)?
- Breathing (eg coughing or wheezing)?

When Did You First Notice The Weight Loss?

Has Your Dog Had Access To Any Toxins?

It is also helpful to know what medications your dog is receiving in regards to the prevention and control of intestinal worms, fleas and heartworm.

Your veterinarian will perform a thorough physical examination of your dog. From the clinical examination and history, a plan can then be formulated for the next step in the diagnostic process. Often a blood, urine or stool sample may be collected to assess your pet's internal organs and general health.

Depending on the condition of your pet and the results from any initial diagnostic tests, further treatment and/or tests may be recommended. This could include admission into hospital for intravenous fluids and appropriate medical treatment, and further diagnostic tests such as radiography and/or ultrasonography.

Causes Of Rapid Weight Loss

Apart from weight loss due to dehydration, rapid weight loss also occurs when your dog has a negative caloric balance. This means that the body is not receiving the necessary calories it needs to maintain a normal weight range. There are several conditions that could cause this including:

- Reduced appetite or intake of calories for some reason (eg severe dental disease can be painful and may prevent your pet from wanting to eat or chew)
- Reduced absorption of calories from the intestine (eg Inflammatory bowel disease can damage the intestinal wall and prevent calories being absorbed into the blood stream)
- Reduced ability to utilise calories due to an underlying medical condition (eg Diabetes Mellitus results in a lack of insulin which means the body is unable to absorb glucose from the blood stream)
- Increased loss of calories (eg vomiting or diarrhoea, renal disease)
- Increased requirement of calories (eg neoplasia)

The examples given are not an exhaustive list of diseases or problems causing rapid weight loss. Your vet will be able to give you more appropriate information and relevant treatment protocols once they have examined your dog and performed the appropriate diagnostic tests.

There are many reasons why a dog can lose weight rapidly so it is important that you take your dog to the vet as soon as you notice unexplained weight loss, as some of these conditions may be serious but many can also be treated successfully, especially if detected early.

It is recommended to visit your vet every 6 months once your dog is aged over 7 years old (which is roughly the equivalent of 50 human years). This allows for early detection and treatment of disease processes that may otherwise lead to weight loss and ill health in your dog.

Weight Loss Tips For Senior Dogs

Older dogs, like older people, have an easier time getting around if they aren't overweight. Losing weight can be a challenge for dogs at any age, but more so as dogs grow older. Still, weight loss for dogs is worth the effort.Slender dogs not only get around more easily, but also actually live longer.A 14-year study showed that dogs fed 25 percent fewer calories than their free-fed littermates lived nearly two years longer, showed fewer visible signs of aging, and enjoyed an extra three years of pain-free mobility before developing canine arthritis.

Health problems that are more common in overweight dogs include pancreatitis, diabetes, heart disease, disc disease, ruptured cruciate ligaments, hip dysplasia, other forms of joint disease, surgical complications, compromised immune systems, and several types of cancer. And sadly, studies show that more than half of America's dogs are overweight – and nearly all of their owners are in denial! If you can't easily feel your dog's ribs and shoulder blades, if her waist is not discernable (a tuck behind the ribs), or if there's a roll of fat at the base of her tail, it's time to face reality and put your dog on a diet.

As WDJ contributor Mary Straus explains, "Because we're so used to seeing overweight dogs, many folks think a dog at his proper weight is too skinny, but as long as the hips and spine are not protruding, and no more than the last rib or two are slightly visible, he's not too thin.If in doubt, ask your vet for an opinion, or go to an agility competition to see what fit dogs look like."

Here Are 10 Tips On How To Help Your Dog Lose Weight:

1. **Feed Your Overweight Dog More Protein And Less Carbohydrates.**

When it comes to weight loss, the ratio of carbohydrates to fats and protein matters more than calories do. Most prescription weight-loss diets are high in carbohydrates, low in fat, and low in protein, a combination that makes it difficult to lose weight.

Dogs thrive on a high-protein diet, which builds lean muscle, and they don't need carbohydrates at all. The ideal canine weight-loss diet is high in protein, low in carbohydrates, and moderate in fat, which satisfies the appetite.

2.   Avoid Feeding Your Dog High-Fiber Foods.

Increased fiber, the indigestible part of carbohydrates, will not help your dog feel satisfied, and too much can interfere with nutrient absorption. Grains are a common source of fiber, and many grain-free foods are high in protein and low in carbs, which can make them effective foods for weight loss (as long as they don't contain too much fat).

3.   Make Your Dog's Food.

Another option is to make your own high-protein, moderate-fat, low-carbohydrate diet

"If you feed a homemade diet, use lean meats, low-fat dairy, and green vegetables in place of most grains and starches," Straus suggests. "Remove the skin from poultry (except for breasts) and remove separable fat from meats. Avoid fatty meats such as lamb, pork, and high-fat beef, or cook them to remove most of the fat. It's okay to include eggs in moderate amounts. You can also use these foods to replace up to 25 percent of a commercial pet food, which will increase the total amount of protein and decrease carbohydrates in the diet.

"There's a common misconception that replacing a large portion of the diet with green beans will help your dog not feel hungry," she adds. "While there's no harm in adding some green beans or other non-starchy veggies to your dog's diet, the extra bulk won't help your dog feel satisfied if you're feeding too few calories or too little fat. It is fat that most helps to satiate your dog; just adding bulk isn't enough. Replacing too much food with green beans can also lead to a protein deficiency, causing the loss of lean muscle rather than fat."

4.   Feed your dog the right fats.

Recent human and canine studies show that the omega-3 fatty acids EPA and DHA from fish oil promote weight loss and help dieters feel more satisfied. Straus recommends giving fish oil that provides 1 to 1.5 mg combined EPA and DHA per pound of body weight daily for healthy dogs, or up to 3 mg for dogs with health problems (such as heart disease, kidney disease, cancer, arthritis, allergies, and other conditions causing inflammation or affecting the immune system). Some cod liver oils, such as Carlson Norwegian Cod Liver Oil with Omega 3s, provide vitamins D and A for additional health benefits.

When adding oils to your dog's diet, keep in mind that oils are pure fat, adding more than 40 calories per teaspoon. Label directions for many liquid fish-oil products are higher than they should be, adding too many calories to your dog's diet. If your dog needs high doses of EPA and DHA, look for more concentrated softgels. Other oils, such as coconut and olive oil, should be carefully measured to be sure you're not adding too much fat.

5.   Reduce your dog's food portion size.

Instead of making drastic changes all at once, cut your dog's food back by about five percent and feed that slightly smaller amount for a week or two. This reduction is about 1 ounce per pound or 1/8 cup per two cups of food. Weigh your dog today and again in one or two weeks. If she doesn't lose weight, reduce the food by another five percent and continue at that amount for one to two weeks. Keep gradually reducing the amount of food until your dog begins to lose weight, then continue feeding that amount.

This strategy helps because reducing the amount of food too suddenly will change your dog's metabolism, making it harder to lose weight and easier to gain it back. Slow, steady weight loss is more likely to result in long-term success.

If you switch to a food that's considerably higher in protein and fat than your current food, cut the quantity by up to one-third, as foods that are more nutrient dense will provide more calories in smaller portions. Even though the total amount your dog receives is less than before, he may be more satisfied.

Weighing Dog Food

Feeding smaller portions more often will help your dog feel less hungry. Replace some dry food with canned or fresh, high-protein food so he thinks he's getting something special. Put his meals in a Kong, Buster Cube, or other food-dispensing toy so he has to work for them, leaving him feeling more satisfied. Freeze his wet food, or dry food mixed with nonfat yogurt, in a Kong toy to make a meal last even longer.

6.   Measure everything your dog eats.

"It's critical to accurately measure your dog's food," says Straus. "I learned the hard way that when I try to eyeball my dogs' food, they gain weight. The only way I've found to achieve consistent weight control is by using an electronic scale to weigh everything I feed. You can find scales at office and kitchen supply stores and online. Most handle up to five pounds with accuracy to one tenth of an ounce, and they can switch to grams for very small measurements."

7. Make your dog's weight loss a family project.

Measuring everything and writing it in your dog's diet book or food log helps family members realize just how much the dog is eating. Feeding a small dinner won't help if Fido is getting breakfast leftovers, afternoon snacks, and training treats all day. Discuss the diet plan with everyone who feeds your dog and get their cooperation. You can give each family member a specific number of small training treats to reward the dog with, and encourage everyone to focus on games, walks, playing fetch, and favorite activities as calorie-free rewards that will keep your dog motivated.

8. Weigh your dog

If your dog is small, you can weigh her on a baby scale or a postal scale designed for packages. Your veterinary clinic has a walk-on scale that accommodates dogs of all sizes, so if your large dog is willing, take her there every one or two weeks. If your dog associates the clinic with unpleasant experiences, use low-calorie, high-value treats to help change her attitude. Most dogs respond well to short visits that include treats, eagerly hopping on the scale, and sitting or standing still for a minute before going home.

"Aim for weight loss of three to five percent of body weight per month, or one percent per week," says Straus. "A 50-pound dog should lose about half a pound per week, or two pounds per month. Once your dog begins losing weight steadily, you can go longer between weigh-ins, but recheck monthly to make sure you're still on track.It's easy to slip back into giving too much food and not notice until your dog has gained back a lot of weight. Caloric needs can also change over time as your dog ages, after neutering, or if his activity level varies seasonally. If you're weighing your dog regularly, you'll be able to catch and correct any weight gain before you have a bigger problem."

9. Rethink The Treats You Feed.

When Ella, her Norwich Terrier, gained weight even with reduced meals, Straus realized that she had to consider the calories Ella received from training treats. "I fed her cooked chicken breast to counter-condition her shyness around strangers that we met on our walks," Straus says. "I put treats in a Kong toy when I had to leave her alone to reduce any anxiety she might feel about my leaving, and I used clicker training to improve my communication with Ella. Altogether, those treats were adding up to a lot of calories."

Fortunately, dogs care more about the number of treats they receive than the size of each treat, so it's more rewarding for a dog to receive several small treats than one big one. For a dog Ella's size, Straus switched to really tiny treats. "I now use treats for nose work training, where I need high-value treats. I cut slices of turkey bacon (17.5 calories per slice) into 35 pieces that are just half a calorie each. Zukes Lil' Links (16 calories each) are cut into 16 pieces, one calorie each. Happy Howie's beef and turkey rolls have 52-60 calories per ounce and can be cut into small cubes of no more than one calorie each (note the lamb variety is much higher in calories). Slice treats in half or quarters lengthwise before dicing to create lots of small pieces."

Treats that are high in fat and calories, such as hot dogs and peanut butter, can pack on the pounds. Instead, try raw baby carrots, zucchini slices, other crunchy vegetables, or small slices of apple, banana, or melon. Make your own treats out of low-fat organ meats like heart or liver. Grapes, raisins, and anything containing xylitol (a sugar substitute) should not be used, as they can be toxic to dogs.

Another strategy is to feed some of your dog's dinner as treats during the day. Just be sure to reduce her meal size accordingly.

10. Find The Right Edible Dog Chew.

Dogs love to chew, and if you can find a low-fat, long-lasting chew, it can keep your dog busy, satisfied, and out of caloric trouble. Dried tendons, steer sticks, and similar chews work well unless they're small enough for the dog to swallow.

If you use rawhide, WDJ recommends high-quality, thick, unbleached (not white) rawhides without added flavorings or smoking, made from one solid piece, and preferably made in the U.S., such as those from Wholesome Hide. See "Finding the Right Rawhide Chew for Your Dog," WDJ May 2009, for information on healthy rawhide chews.

Fresh, raw bones can also be used for chewing, but Straus adds an important caveat, "Bones, like any hard chew, have the potential to break teeth, particularly in older dogs whose teeth are more brittle. Bones that are too big for dogs to get between their molars and chomp down on, such as knuckles, are less likely to cause problems than marrow bones, which are filled with fat and therefore not a good choice."

Creating A Weight Reduction Plan For Dogs

Weight loss is tough for anyone - two- or four-legged! However, losing weight and getting in shape can not only add not years to your dog's life, but it can also make those extra years more enjoyable. Helping your cuddly canine to shed a few pounds may be easier than you think. It simply requires a commitment to weight loss and fitness, attention to details, and the assistance of your veterinary healthcare team.

Why Should My Dog Lose Weight?

dog_obesity_2017-02As few as five pounds above the ideal body weight can put your dog at risk for developing some serious medical conditions. Unfortunately, when a dog is overweight or obese it no longer is a question of if your dog will develop a condition secondary to the excess weight but how soon and how serious. Some of the common disorders associated with excess weight include:

- Type 2 diabetes
- Heart disease
- Osteoarthritis (arthritis)
- Increased frequency of joint injuries

- High blood pressure

- Some forms of cancer - especially intra-abdominal cancers

Overweight and obese dogs usually have shorter lives than their fitter, normal weight counterparts. Heavy dogs tend to physically interact less with their families and are less energetic and playful.Because they tend to lie around more, it is easier to overlook early signs of illness, since we may attribute their lethargy to their normal laziness.There is good evidence that dogs who are a healthy weight live significantly longer than dogs who are overweight.

How Should I Begin A Weight Loss Program For My Dog?

Theoretically, weight loss seems simple enough: fewer calories in plus more calories out equals weight loss.Unfortunately, it is not as simple as that.

You should never put your dog on a diet without the assistance of your veterinary healthcare team. There may be an underlying medical condition that is causing or contributing to your dog's excess weight. Some common diseases associated with weight gain include hypothyroidism and hyperadrenocorticism

(Cushing's disease). These diseases, along with others, should be eliminated as possible causes or contributors to your dog's weight problem prior to beginning a diet. Too many dogs start on a diet and fail to lose weight simply because the diet was not the problem - a disease was. Your veterinarian will perform a physical examination and recommend blood tests to ensure that there are no obstacles to weight loss for your pet.

How Much Should I Feed My Dog To Promote Weight Loss?

In order to answer this question, your veterinarian will need to calculate your dog's ideal weight based on its breed and size. Based on your dog's degree of excess weight, your veterinarian may recommend a target weight higher than the ideal weight to start. After the dog loses this weight, a re-evaluation will be made to determine whether further weight loss is needed.A safe weight loss for most dogs is 3-5% body weight loss per month.

If you are using a reducing diet obtained from your veterinarian, the calorie content odog_scalef the food will be on the label, and a member of your veterinary healthcare team will help you determine the appropriate amount to feed. If you choose to use an alternate source of food, and this information is not available on the label, you will need to contact the manufacturer to get it.

What Makes Veterinary Weight Loss Diets Special?

There are a number of weight control diets available at pet stores that work well for a dog who only needs to lose a small amount of weight. However, these diets are often not as effective as veterinary weight loss diets if a dog needs to lose a significant amount of weight or if your dog has other medical conditions.

Not all weight loss strategies work for every dog, so there are many different diets to address this. Some weight loss diets, such as Purina Proplan OM® and Royal Canin® Calorie Control, are high protein, low carbohydrate, others such as Royal Canin® Satiety and Hills® Prescription Diet w/d have high fiber content to help your dog feel more full and stop begging for food. Some newer weight loss diets, such as Hills® Prescription Diet Metabolic, use specific nutrients that can promote increased metabolism, helping dogs burn calories more quickly. Your veterinarian will be able to advise the best weight loss diet for your dog's particular situation.

How quickly Should I Introduce The New Reducing Diet To My Dog?

When you are introducing a new diet to your dog, you should allow about a week to make the transition. To minimize digestive upsets, mix the new diet in with the old diet in gradually increasing proportions. Start by feeding ¼ of the new diet mixed with ¾ of the old diet for one to two days, then increase to half-and-half for another two days, then ¾ new food and ¼ old food for a final two to three days before completely switching to the new diet.

"To minimize digestive upsets, mix the old and new diets together in gradually increasing proportions."To enhance the palatability of the diet food, try warming the food, adding a flavoring such as a small amount of salmon juice, low-fat chicken or beef broth, or an omega-3 fatty acid supplement.

How Can I Get My Dog To Lose More Weight Through Exercise?

The first thing you can do to help your dog lose weight is to increase the intensity and length of your daily walk. Few dogs will naturally walk at a pace that generates the elevated heart rates needed for sustained aerobic activity and weight loss.

Based on observations of people walking with their dogs, the average pace is 20 to 25 minutes per mile (12-15 minutes per kilometer), which is actually a stroll. They make frequent pauses (on average every one to two minutes) to allow their dog to smell an interesting object or mark territory. Walking for weight loss is very different than walking for pleasure. You should aim for a daily brisk 30-minute walk. With this sort of walking, you should break into a slight sweat within a few minutes. For details on developing a healthy walking program for your dog, "Increase the intensity and length of your daily walk."

Dog_fetch_1Some additional simple tips for getting your dog to exercise more are:

Move the food bowl upstairs or downstairs, changing its location frequently so that the dog always has to walk to get to its food bowl. Overweight dogs are smart dogs and if the food bowl moves upstairs, they will head upstairs, too.

Feed your dog in a treat ball or puzzle feeder to slow down ingestion and help them feel more full.

Use toys, balls, laser pointers, squeaky toys, or sticks to encourage games of chase or fetch. Try to play with your dog for at least ten to fifteen minutes twice a day. There are toys that move randomly and make noises that may also be interesting to your dog. For many dogs, variety is important, and what is exciting or interesting today may be boring tomorrow.

How Often Should I Have My Dog's Progress Checked?

After you have put your dog on a weight loss program, it is critical that you determine if it is working for your dog. In general, your dog should be weighed at least every month until the ideal weight is achieved. Each dog is an individual and may require adjustments in the recommended diet or routine before finding the correct approach. If there is no significant weight loss in one month, (3-5% of the starting body weight), then the program will need to be modified. Sometimes, making only a slight change can deliver significant improvements.

It is often easier to give in to the dog that wakes you at four in the morning to be fed or the dog that stares at you during dinner or television time until you relent. These dogs have trained us well and know exactly which buttons to press when it comes to getting their way. Here are some tips for handling your pleading pup:

- Do not use a self-feeder. While this seems obvious, auto-feeders are nothing more than unlimited candy machines to a fat dog.

- If you do use an automatic feeder, use one that opens with a timer.This way you can measure out the proper amount and divide it into daily meals.

- Pet your dog or play with him when he begs for food. Many dogs substitute food for affection so flip the equation and you may find that playtime displaces mealtime.

- Go for a walk with your dog when he begs.The distraction and interaction may be just enough to make him forget his desire for food.

- Feed small meals frequently - especially give a last feeding for those dogs that like to wake you up in the wee hours begging for more goodies - divide the total volume or calories into four to six smaller meals - whatever you do, do not feed extra food.

- When the bowl is empty and your dog is pleading, add a few kibbles to the bowl. A few means only a few - not a handful. Keep a few kibbles separate from your dog's measured daily ration for this purpose.

If more than one person is feeding your dog, you should measure out the total daily food into a separate container such as a covered food storage container.Then, everybody knows how much the dog has been fed, and how much is left for the day.If you enjoy giving treats to your dog, feed her several kibbles from the container rather than giving her high calorie dog biscuits.

Give a couple of pieces of vegetables such as baby carrots, frozen sliced carrots, broccoli, green beans, celery, or asparagus. Most dogs love crunchy treats so make it a healthy and low-calorie choice. Do not give meat treats or carbohydrate treats such as bread or pasta. Even small amounts of these can lead to weight gain in dogs prone to obesity.

Offer fresh water instead of food. If your dog is eyeing the empty food bowl, a drink of cold, fresh water may satisfy the craving.

The ideal solution for multi-dog households is to feed the dogs separately. Feed the overweight dog his diet in one room while feeding the other dog its food elsewhere.After a prescribed time, generally fifteen to thirty minutes, remove any uneaten food.

"The ideal solution for multi-dog households is to feed the dogs separately."

Do not leave food out while you are away from home. You cannot control who eats what when you are not around.

How Long Will My Dog Need To Be On A Diet?

Most dogs will achieve their ideal weight within six to eight months. If the process is taking longer than this, something needs to be changed. A healthy weight loss is between one to five pounds per month based on your dog's size and current condition. Some dogs may need to go slower while others may shed the pounds more quickly.

For most dogs, the secret to weight loss is a dedicated, committed, and concerned family. Dogs do not understand that their excess weight is causing them harm. It is up to us as good stewards to protect them from harm and not inadvertently contribute to their premature death or development of debilitating diseases. Together, you and your veterinary healthcare team can help your dog achieve a healthy body weight and condition safely and successfully.

How To Make Homemade Dog Food To Lose Weight

Start With The Healthiest Protein You Can Find

About 50 percent of your dog's diet should consist of lean animal protein, including skinless chicken or turkey, eggs, low-fat dairy products such as cottage cheese, and fish.Fish can be fresh or canned, but if you're feeding canned fish, make sure it has no added oil, as this can increase the calorie content considerably. Protein can be cooked or raw, but if you're cooking, make sure you're not using any oils, which increase calorie count. Try varying the protein so your dog is eating two to three types each week, making it more likely he'll obtain all necessary nutrients and prevent palate boredom.

Vary Your Other Ingredients

Dogs can lose weight eating non-starchy vegetables and whole grains, but grains cause allergies in some dogs, so start with small amounts and increase only if you notice no side effects. Puree cooked healthy veggies such as pumpkin, spinach, kale and other leafy greens, and mix them with the protein. They provide lots of fiber, which will help your dog feel full without adding tons of calories - an excellent compromise for weight loss. To keep the calorie count low, steam, bake or boil all ingredients, either together or separately.

Other Benefits

A low-calorie, low-fat homemade diet has many benefits. Because you can control what goes into a homemade diet, you can make sure your dog is not getting additives and preservatives. You can prepare homemade diets to be free of soy, wheat, corn, dairy and high-fat meats such as beef. These ingredients are not only high in calories and sugars which means they contribute to weight gain but they can also cause allergies and a number of problems in dogs.

A Word of Caution

Commercial diets have been designed to provide dogs with all the nutrients they need for good health. Homemade diets, meanwhile, run the risk of being deficient in certain nutrients, including zinc, vitamins D and E, copper and essential fatty acids. The only way to ensure that your pet is getting everything he needs is to talk to your vet and to make sure you feed a variety of foods of the highest quality possible.

Recipes For Overweight Or Obese Dogs

Understanding a dog's dietary needs can be complex, but there are some general guidelines you can take into account. Before starting to cook, you'll need to know the proportion of nutrients that should be included in a dog's meals regardless of its weight:

- Animal protein: 50%

- Vegetables: 30%

- Carbohydrates (cereals, potatoes): 20%

The best low-fat recipes for overweight or obese dogs are the following:

Potatoes and beef stew: Simply cook the potatoes, beef and carrots respecting the cooking times of each ingredient. If you want to make it tastier you can add olive oil, but with a sprayer to avoid an excessive amount.

Chicken with rice and vegetables: Boil the rice along with a handful of spinach, carrots and tomatoes. Meanwhile, grill a low-fat cut of chicken breast, chop it and mix it with the rice.

Potatoes with hake: Cut the potatoes into thin slices and put them in the oven with a little water for about 15 minutes.

Before the potatoes finish cooking, add the hake fillets without skin.

Mix of vegetables with ham: Boil potatoes, spinach, carrots and leeks. Then, tear the ham to bits and and mix it in. You can sauté the mixture slightly to make it tastier.

Pasta with tuna and tomato: Crush a tomato and fry it with a little oil. Then boil the pasta and mix it with the tomato sauce. Finally you can add some canned tuna, but it must be natural, without oil and salt.

Mashed potatoes with salmon: This recipe includes healthy fats, which are not harmful if consumed moderately and through quality food. Boil the potatoes, drain them and add very little oil.Then, mash them. Steam the boneless salmon fillet or bake it in its own juices.

Your dog should eat 3 times a day (breakfast, lunch and dinner) and do so in moderate amounts. Besides following a proper diet, an overweight or obese dog must perform daily physical exercise.Take it for outdoor walks and play games, or even join a dynamic dog sport.

More Healthy Homemade Dog Food Recipes

Many dog owners find preparing homemade dog food to be highly rewarding.Watching your dog thrive and knowing exactly what he's eating can be reassuring.So if you have the time and inclination, homemade dog food may be a great option for your pooch.

For this reason, I would like to show you how to make your own dog food.My dog food recipes are easy, cost-effective and nutritionally balanced. They can also work wonders in helping to manage your dog's weight. (Sorry, sausages and peanut butter dog treats are not suitable for dieting dogs!)

Nutrition And Calories In Homemade Dog Food

Each of my dog food recipes lists its protein and calorie content. If you have an overweight dog, and know your dog's daily calorie requirements these homemade dog food recipes make it easy to count calories.

Many homemade dog food recipes are not nutritionally balanced.Over time this can lead to serious developmental disorders and health issues.

What You Should Know About Homemade Dog Food

Homemade dog food is prone to rapid bacterial and fungal growth if it is not chilled. Refrigerate or freeze your prepared homemade dog food in sealed containers at less than 4 degrees Celsius (32-39.2 degrees Fahrenheit).

- Use refrigerated homemade dog food within 3 days. Check for odor and color changes before serving. Serve at just below body temperature. Ensure there are no hot spots if defrosting or warming the food in a microwave.

- Homemade dog food must be supplemented with calcium and dog vitamin and mineral powders.These dog supplements are not optional.

- Each recipe provides 1000 kcal. Serving size is determined by your dog's dieting calorie requirement.

- Measure out the ingredients using kitchen scales to ensure the protein and calorie content is accurate.

- Do not cook or heat the vitamin/mineral supplement. Instead, add it to the meal just before feeding.

1. **Chicken, Rice and Vegetable Homemade Dog Food**

Nutrient Analysis: This recipe provides 1000 kcal and 76 g protein.

Note: Ingredient weights refer to raw weights.

Ingredients

- Chicken breast (skinless) 290g (10oz)
- Brown rice 145g (5oz)
- Broccoli 46g (1.6 oz)
- Carrots 46g (1.6 oz)
- Peas 46 g (1.6 oz)
- Extra virgin olive oil 2 ½ teaspoons
- Psyllium Powder 2 tablespoons

Method:

- Cook rice until tender- follow packet guidelines.
- Steam broccoli, carrots and peas until just tender.
- Cook chicken- Steam, microwave or use non-stick pan to oven bake.
- Dice cooked chicken and vegetables

- Mix chicken and vegetables with cooked rice.

- Add 2 1/2 teaspoons of extra virgin olive oil.

- Add 2 level tablespoons of psyllium powder.

- Weigh final product and portion according to your dog's dieting calorie intake.

- Prior to serving, add a dog vitamin and mineral supplement prior to serving.

- Or alternatively add: 1/4 teaspoon iodised salt, 1 x crushed 25 mg zinc tablet, 1500 mg calcium, 1 crushed multi-vitamin tablet (Centrum women). Mix it thoroughly through food and serve.

Homemade Dog Food Recipes

Know the calorie count of all ingredients in your homemade dog food recipes

2. Tuna and Vegetable Homemade Dog Food

Nutrient Analysis: This recipe provides 1000 kcal and 149g protein.

Note: Ingredient weights refer to raw weights.

Ingredients:

- Canned tuna in water or brine, drained (577 grams/ 20.4 oz)
- Potato, scrubbed or peeled (288 grams/ 10.2 oz)
- Cauliflower (138 grams/ 4.9 oz)
- Green beans (138 grams/ 4.9 oz)
- Extra virgin olive oil (2 ½ teaspoons)
- Psyllium powder (1 tablespoon)

Method:

- Steam vegetables until tender.
- Dice and mix vegetables.
- Break up tinned tuna and mix evenly through cooked vegetables.
- Add 2 ½ teaspoons extra virgin olive oil.
- Add 1 level tablespoon of psyllium powder.
- Weigh cooked product and portion according to your dog's dieting calorie intake.
- Before serving, add mineral and vitamin supplements: Use a dog vitamin and mineral supplement suitable for home cooking. Or alternatively add:1/4 teaspoon iodised salt, 1 x crushed 25 mg zinc tablet, 1500 mg calcium, 1 crushed multi-vitamin tablet (Centrum women).

- Mix evenly though food prior to serving.

Things To Consider When Creating Homemade Dog Food Recipes

Before creating your own homemade dog food recipes, ask yourself the following questions:

- Will you be able to accurately determine the calories in you dog food recipes? Human dieting apps such as My Fitness Pal will allow you to breakdown the calorie count of individual ingredients.
- Will you be able to ensure correct nutrient ratios in your dog food recipes, e.g. calcium and phosphorus ratios?
- Can you provide the essential nutrient components in your dog food recipes? This can be very difficult to achieve without the aid of specially prepared supplements.
- Have you factored in the cost and availability of the ingredients in your dog food recipes? Substituting ingredients when there is short supply alters the nutritional balance and calorie content of the recipe.

- Have you ensured that the ingredients are safe for dogs? Some human foods are toxic to dogs. For more information read foods poisonous to dogs.

- Have you considered the possibility of selective eating (where your dog refuses to eat some of the ingredients) such as spitting out the peas? This will alter your dog's calorie intake and nutrient balance. Avoid selective eating by blending the finished product.

- Have you considered the preparation and cooking time involved in your dog food recipes?

- Have you considered the storage life of homemade dog food and the need for refrigeration or freezing?

The successful preparation of healthy homemade dog food recipes requires planning and attention to detail.

Conclusion

Many diets can help your dog lose weight.

Some of the most well-researched diets and eating plans include intermittent fasting, plant-based diets, low-carb diets, low-fat diets, the paleo diet, the Mediterranean diet, WW (Weight Watchers), and the DASH diet. While all of the above diets have been shown to be effective for weight loss, the diet you choose should depend on your dogs lifestyle and food preferences. This ensures that you are more likely to stick to it in the long term.